Insight: A Study of Proverbs

The Ability to Choose the Right Path in Life

by Dennis Carrow

ONESTONE
BIBLICAL RESOURCES

Published by:
One Stone Press
979 Lovers Lane
Bowling Green, KY 42103

Printed in the United States of America

ISBN 10: 1-941422-01-2
ISBN 13: 978-1-941422-01-4

Supplemental Materials Available:
PowerPoint slides for each lesson
Answer key
Downloadable PDF

ONE STONE
BIBLICAL RESOURCES

www.onestone.com

INTRODUCTION
The Wisdom that Comes from God

What are proverbs?

Instruction given in proverbial form is one of the most ancient forms of teaching. Simply stated, proverbs are sayings or sentences of ethical wisdom. The most appropriate definition is expressed in the following: **"A word fitly spoken is like apples of gold in a picture of silver"** *(Proverbs 25:11). View the book of Proverbs as a map that foretells your journey through life. Clearly marked are the reflective signs of danger. Examine them, memorize their size, shape, and the meaning of each marking. Some reflect the obstacles that you must overcome, while others point to pitfalls and chasms that must be avoided at all costs, for they will swallow your soul. Others offer gracious instructions that fill the heart with confidence, courage, and vision.*

Our life experiences from youth to adulthood expose us to many forms of deception. The first time we experience betrayal by a friend or are taken advantage of, we experience a pain and emotion that can alter our outlook and enjoyment of life. We become confused by activity that our peers present as fun, only to discover that, after being lured into that activity, it brings embarrassment and regret. Wouldn't it be wonderful to be aware of those painful pitfalls in advance so we could avoid them? God has provided the knowledge that informs us of those perils in life. Accompanying these instructions are sayings that, if assimilated into our hearts, will bring joy, enthusiasm, and a love for life that others may only dream about. God guides us in every endeavor we pursue in this life with dignity, honor, moral character, and guiltless innocence.

A powerful weapon Satan uses against us as we grow in Christ is the accusation that being a Christian makes us naive. He wants nothing more than to lower our self-image to that of a gullible wimp. We can be tricked into thinking a Christ-centered life will cause us to miss out on all this life has to offer. This perception is based upon a worldly view that one must experience something in order to comprehend it. We have heard people talk of some immoral or illegal act with arrogance and pride. Their boldness may have impressed you and caused you to wonder what it would be like to do such a thing. It may be, because of this kind of thinking, you have engaged in some immoral activity, only to suffer the pain of regret and the embarrassment that accompanies foolish behavior. Prisons, homes for unwed mothers, and cemeteries are full of individuals who have wished they had known what the result of their actions would be before they did them. Peer pressure and an obscured view of worldly activity will lead us to dishonor our lives and destroy our plans for the future.

The fact we are tempted to do wrong should be of no surprise. *All that is in the world* are the things that tempt us (1 John 2:16). Being tempted is not sinful. We sin when we make uninformed or foolish decisions to do the wrong thing. (James 1:14-16). Appropriate decisions are based upon knowledge of righteousness and a willingness to make proper application of that knowledge. It is the proper application of knowledge that gives birth to **wisdom**. It is in our search for this wisdom that we embark upon this study of the book of Proverbs. Because pain and sorrow accompany wrong decisions, our approach toward this study has a real purpose. God, through these inspired writings, will define wisdom and provide insight into how we are to apply it in our lives. The result of this study is to enable us to avoid those foolish things that bring pain to ourselves, embarrassment to our families, and most importantly, separation from our Lord.

God chose the medium of the Scriptures to communicate to us. Realizing God is our Creator, He alone knows what is best for us. Let us accept His word as truth, receive His word with gladness, and allow it to affect our lives in such a way that we might enjoy the abundant life promised us in Jesus Christ. (1 Thessalonians 2:13; John 10:10). While we may readily accept the abundant life in Christ as a concept, when exposed to the influence of the world, we can lose sight of what God's "perfect plan" is for our life. May we ever hold God's eternal light before us. Let us learn from God today those precepts and principles that will prepare us for tomorrow. We must refuse to allow Satan to rob us of the life that now is, and the one that is to come.

To properly prepare our minds for this study, meditate on these words of Solomon from the book of Ecclesiastes, "Remove sorrow from thy heart, and put away evil from your eyes...remember your Creator in the days of your youth" (Ecclesiastes 11:10-12:1). The instructions are to enjoy living and realize we are not to go forward without restraint or instruction. How does remembering God relate to enjoying life? Does this only mean that we have some mental image of His existence? No! It is to acknowledge Him as the One who has given us not only our physical existence but a spirit that is in need of His guidance and direction. It is to accept His word as the source of all truth. While some view the Bible as a book of obscure religious doctrine that has little relevance to their lives, the Scriptures provide everything man needs to know about life and abundant living. (2 Peter 1:3). In our study of Proverbs, **God will communicate what He wants every person to know today—about tomorrow.**

Our relationship with God is founded upon our knowledge of Him. As we receive His instruction in wisdom He will in turn bless us, and we will express to God our recognition of His majesty and our gratitude to Him for the direction He has given to our lives. May our hearts be filled with thanksgiving for the gift of life. May we develop a desire to honor and obey Him in all things, a regret for past indiscretions, and a sincere willingness **to perceive the words of understanding and to receive the instruction of wisdom, justice, judgment, and equity.**

――――――――――――――――――

Foundational principle:

A wise man does not think he knows everything! (Proverbs 1:2-6)

Table of Contents

Where We Begin: The Fear of the Lord

Getting focused

It is understood that God is the fountain from which all wisdom flows. The early portion of chapter one points out that you possess ability to assimilate wisdom. Realize wisdom is present whether we accept it and make application of it or not. Therefore, you determine if you will become wise or live foolishly. God is the ultimate source of all things, but your personal decision to receive these words of wisdom will determine the outcome of this study.

God has promised wisdom to those who, by faith, seek it (James 1:5-7). Therefore, we must first focus on this single fact: **the fear of the Lord is the beginning of wisdom** (Job 28:12-15, 20-28).

Godly instruction vs. sinful enticement
Read Proverbs 1:7-9, 10-19, 20-23

A common mistake made as we mature is the failure to recognize the benefit of listening to those who care about us. Following the affirmation of God as the source of wisdom, we are taught to receive the instruction of our father and mother (v. 8). Experience will provide knowledge.

Verses 7-9 display the adorning effect when we obey the commands to honor our father and mother (Exodus 20:12; Ephesians 6:2). Making application of this brings a blessing and honor to our lives.

A contrast is drawn between the two roads in life we can travel. One is that of discretion, understanding, and all that is good. The other is the enticement to engage in things that are motivated by selfish greed. We will encounter both in our lives. Wisdom is determined by the road we choose to travel.

- **Wisdom cries out**...I will make known my words to you (vs. 20-23).

- **Sinners entice**...come with us, we shall fill our houses with precious possessions (vs. 11-14).

Fear, in one sense, is defined as the "instinctive emotion aroused by impending or seeming danger" (New Webster's Dictionary).

While this emotion will cause one to tremble at the power of God, **fear also means to "stand in awe" or respect.** Both definitions must be applied to the beginning of wisdom.

The fear of the Lord is one that will bring us to **love and worship Him** as the Almighty Creator.

Memorize and meditate

"My son, if sinners entice you do not consent."

- Proverbs 1:10

In contrast, a great social ill is disrespect, which leads to a disregard for authority.

The failure in rejecting wisdom
Read Proverbs 1:24-33

The New Testament principle, "God is not mocked, whatsoever a man sows, that shall he also reap," (Galatians 6:7) is clearly brought to light in this text. The result of rejecting God is certain. When trouble comes, the cry of those who have rejected Him will fall prey to their own deception. The rejection of the truth leads to delusion and confusion.

The text does not imply that God rejects men who come to a knowledge of the truth and repent, but those who have lost sight of reality by rejecting His word (consider Romans 1:20-22, 28). This passage expresses our personal responsibility and the power to choose. Those rejected by God are those who rejected Him (vs. 24-25, 29, 31).

The opening statement of verse 5, **"the wise man will hear,"** holds the key to the promises of peace, protection, contentment, and happiness made at the conclusion of this chapter. These things come only to those who listen.

Questions to consider

1. What determines the difference between the foolish and the wise? _____

   _____

2. What criminal activity today mirrors that mentioned in verse 14?_____

   _____

3. What is the response of the wise to those who attempt to involve us in things that are wrong? _____

   _____

4. Why will God not answer those in trouble in verses 28-30?_____

   _____

5. In light of the things God has revealed in this study, how will you respond in prayer to Him? _____

   _____

The Storehouse for Wisdom: A Good and Honest Heart

Getting focused

Regardless of the amount of knowledge we gain from God's word, it can easily be taken away from us if we fail to keep it in the proper place. Satan attempts to rob us of wisdom by inserting things that deviate from God's instruction. Some refuse to receive God's word, but for those who have accepted the truth, Satan repeatedly attempts to sow seeds of doubt. This lures us away from God by causing us to think we are missing something while walking in the light of God's word.

The only place you can protect the wisdom you receive from God is by hiding it in a good and honest heart. This requires some preparation on our part.

The prerequisite to obtaining wisdom from God
Read Proverbs 2:1-9

First, we must recognize ourselves as children of God. The identity crises we often experience could be avoided by this simple acknowledgment. The attitude that will bring wisdom and understanding can be summarized in one word: **desire!** If we:

- Receive and value the commands (v. 1)

- Listen and apply wisdom and understanding (v. 2)

- Diligently seek to make proper decisions (v. 3)

- Search for truth above all else (v. 4)

Then, we will receive understanding and knowledge (v. 5).

The effect of the wisdom of God in your heart
Read Proverbs 2:10-22

When we adopt the proper attitude toward God and His word He transforms our life. Those foolish things we may have once engaged in no longer burden us. The knowledge and wisdom from God brings comfort and confidence.

We can rest assured if we have purposed in our heart to know and to do God's will—**we can.**

There is no reason to ever doubt that we can be victorious in our quest to **wisely discern, understand, and apply** God's word in our lives. We can receive the **abundant life** and the **spiritual blessings** He offers to us!

Wisdom is the **relationship** we are seeking to have with knowledge.

Memorize and meditate

"Discretion will preserve you; understanding will keep you."

- Proverbs 2:11

When we find ourselves in situations that call for quick decisions regarding a moral question, the wisdom acquired from God gives us the ability to make the right decision before we make the wrong decision.

Let us look ahead and perceive those who would deceive us or mislead us. Wisdom allows us to apply the knowledge that will prevent us from being deceived by those who live godless lives. A life without God is the road that leads to a point of no return. We must hide our purity and innocence within our hearts. It must be protected from those who wish to take it from us.

A contrast is shown between the condition of those who make wise decisions and those who make foolish ones. The two roads in life are the one with the good men and the one of the transgressor (vs. 20, 22)

Similar to Jesus's sermon on the mount, the morally courageous shall inherit the earth. (Matthew 5:5) Does Jesus imply the nature of our inheritance is more than eternity in heaven?

Questions to consider

1. Identify and discuss five things required in order to obtain wisdom.

    1. _____

    2. _____

    3. _____

    4. _____

    5. _____

2. How can we prevent being led down the road with the unrighteous?_____
    _____
    _____

3. Define moral courage._____
    _____
    _____

The Benefits of Wisdom: Character, Confidence and Contentment

Getting focused

The writer introduces numerous benefits in receiving instruction from God, in contrast to the destructive effects of ignorance and foolishness. The blessed life of a disciple of the Lord is remarkable. List all of the things that you hope to get out of life, then compare it with what wisdom will deliver.

- Long life (vs. 2, 16)
- Favor and high esteem (v. 4)
- Health and strength (v. 8)
- Material blessings (v. 10)
- Happiness, rest and peace (vs. 17, 18, 24)
- Deliverance from trouble (vs. 25, 26)
- Eternal life (v. 35)

Trust in the Lord and He will direct and bless your life
Read Proverbs 3:1-10

If we will accept the teachings of the Lord, we can avoid many of the hurtful, destructive ways of the world. Walking by the precepts of God establishes us as people of character. The result of being upright is:

- **Physical health:** a lifestyle that is conducive to healthy living

- **Mental strength:** self-esteem and peace of mind resulting from a clear conscience

- **Material blessing:** the proper attitude toward possessions which enables you to use your resources wisely

There are times in life when you will want to "do your own thing." The words of verses five through seven should be committed to our memory: "Trust in the Lord with all your heart and lean not to your own understanding. In all your ways acknowledge Him, and He will direct your paths. Do not be wise in your own eyes. Fear the Lord and depart from evil."

Remember: Our purpose of gaining wisdom is to learn how to **make the right decisions** in our life, without **having to experience** those things that are wrong.

The essence of the wisdom of God: The ability to make the right decision **before** we make the wrong decision.

Memorize and meditate

"The Lord will be your confidence, and keep your foot from being caught."

- Proverbs 3:26

Simply stated, when faced with the choice of whether or not to do something you feel is right but contradicts what God says—**trust in the Lord's way.**

Some lessons are not easily learned, but the result is priceless peace
Read Proverbs 3:11-18

Verses 11 and 12 have caused some to wonder how one can be chastened by the Lord. I believe this refers to the conscience that is sensitive to God's will, through His word, and suffers guilt when His instructions have been violated. The sensation of guilt is not pleasant to experience but produces a peaceful spiritual existence when we are corrected by our heavenly Father (Hebrews 12:5-11).

The creative power of wisdom
Read Proverbs 3:19-26

When introduced to the power of wisdom, we learn the foundation of creation is established and founded in the wisdom of God. When we examine this in light of other Scripture, we comprehend the wisdom of God to be the word of God. "The worlds were framed by the word of God" (Hebrews 11:3).

The knowledge imparted by God makes us a new creation, contrary to those who walk about without hope. The very power that created all things now guides and directs our lives. Creation declares His eternal power (Romans 1:20).

Share that which God gives with others
Read Proverbs 3:19-26

The manifestation of the power of God's word is seen in how it works in our life. We learn that the blessings we receive through making application of verses 9 and 10 are to be utilized in helping those less fortunate. A fundamental principle in obtaining and maintaining the wisdom of God is through recognizing that it is more blessed to give than to receive. The result of this principle is peace with our fellow man (vs. 29-30). Though some may seem to prosper by taking advantage of others, they have no fellowship with God—thus, no real happiness.

The grace extended to us by God is based upon our humility. If someone is not willing to live by God's precepts and principles, they will not receive spiritual blessings from God.

Questions to consider

1. Discuss some benefits you have received by making application of wisdom in your life. _____
    _____
    _____
    _____

2. What is the result of rejecting God's instruction? _____
    _____
    _____

3. What do we learn in verse 3 about the nature of wisdom? _____
    _____
    _____

4. Explain how we bind God's commands around our neck and write them on the tablets of our heart. _____
    _____
    _____

5. How can a person lose wisdom? _____
    _____
    _____

The Effects of Wisdom: Preservation and Deliverance

Getting focused

Some very profound revelations are made in this chapter concerning the function or role that wisdom will play in our lives. The priority and supremacy of obtaining wisdom is expressed by the statement, "wisdom is the principal thing." As we have observed in previous lessons, the purpose of wisdom is to enable us to avoid making foolish decisions before we actually experience them. This leads the inspired writer to teach us the importance of putting first things first.

As we turn to God for wisdom He will return to us many blessings. Many of these blessings are discussed now. It is important in this stage of our study that we fully recognize the effect and blessings we receive from taking God at His word.

First things first—listen, learn, and live
Read Proverbs 4:1-9

The repeated admonition, "hear my children," is given as the introduction to the ensuing instructions. This admonition is given again in verses 20-22. The motivation for laying hold of wisdom is seen in the positive results she brings.

- **Love her**, she will preserve and keep.

- **Exalt her**, she will promote, honor, graciously adorn, and deliver.

The instruction we receive from God must be given a preeminent place in our heart. If we think highly of or love someone, we find ourselves thinking of them often. This must be our attitude toward the instructions given by God though His word.

Learning from the past clears the path to the future
Read Proverbs 4:10-13

Verse 11 speaks of the instructions that have been given in days gone by. It is because of this the future looks bright

> "Wisdom is the **principal** thing; therefore get wisdom. And in all your getting, get understanding."
>
> - Proverbs 4:7

and unimpeded. The essence of the future is based upon our holding to instruction.

Through applying wisdom, our lives will not be cut short due to foolish decisions or careless activities.

The blinding effects of darkness
Read Proverbs 4:14-19

In contrast to the sweet sleep discussed in Proverbs 3:24, wickedness obstructs rest. Also depicted in this text is the consuming effect of evil. Consider Jesus' description of those who follow Him in Matthew 5:14—"Those who walk in the light are as a city set on a hill, whose light cannot be hid"—in contrast to the wicked, stumbling in darkness all the days of their life. Though they may find temporary joy, when they look to the future there is nothing there!

Pursuits in life begin from within
Read Proverbs 4:20-27

Our heart involves our intellect, emotion, and volition. The attributes of the spiritual heart are utilized for thought (23:7), meditation (19:14), reason (Mark 2:6, 8), understanding (Matthew 13:15), and serving (Deuteronomy 10:12). The emotional aspect is exercised in love (Matthew 13:15) and sorrow (Romans 9:2). It is through our personal examination of our own actions that we know our heart (1 John 3:19-21).

The condition of your heart will determine the wisdom of your walk in life. The parable of the sower illustrates perfectly who will retain wisdom and honor (Luke 8:11-18).

What we say is a reflection of what is in our heart. To control the tongue is to begin to gain control of the heart (Matthew 15:18; James 3).

We must look straight ahead and remain focused. It is essential that we consider the direction we are heading today. We can and must know we are walking in the light of truth. If we are not, we must respond by moving into the light.

Memorize and meditate

"Keep your heart with all diligence, for out of it spring the issues of life."

- Proverbs 4:23

Questions to consider

1. Explain how wisdom can preserve or extend your life. _____

   _____

   _____

   _____

2. How are honor and grace created by wisdom?_____

   _____

   _____

   _____

3. What is the relationship between what we say and what is in our heart? _____

   _____

   _____

   _____

The Blinding Nature of Immorality: The Dangers of Indecency

Getting focused

When God created man He saw that it was not good for him to be alone. Thus, God created woman to be his companion. They are to be heirs together in the grace of life (1 Peter 3:7). The relationship between a man and a woman is perfect in design because it originated in the mind of God. However, men can pervert the beauty of God's plan by failing to live within the framework of God's design.

Marriage is honorable among all, and the bed undefiled (Hebrews 13:4). The marriage relationship is the bond ordained, established, and witnessed by God through which men and women enter into a unique relationship. It is within the confines of this relationship that man can satisfy his romantic desires. Sin, sadness, and pain have been the result of young men and women failing to listen to God's words of wisdom concerning their relationship with each other.

Immorality robs innocence and takes away honor
Read Proverbs 5

As penetrating as a two-edged sword, the deceptive influence of immoral people separate us from reason and understanding. Verse 23 tells us that if we become involved in immorality we will be caught up or trapped by it. The result is spiritual death and a confused emotional state that leads one farther and farther from the truth.

We can detect those who are immoral by listening to the activities they plan (v. 5).

We must find satisfaction and fulfillment through the lawful provisions instructed by God's word. We protect our honor by refusing to have any relationship other than those allowed by God.

"[An adulteress] does not ponder the **path of life**; her ways are **unstable**, she does not know it."

- Proverbs 5:6

The tragic result in failing to do this is:

- Loss of honor (v. 9)

- Loss of possessions (v. 10)

- Loss of purity and possible infection with disease (v. 11)

- Public humiliation (vs. 12-14)

- Loss of direction and spiritual death (vs. 22-23)

The instruction we receive from God must be given a preeminent place in our heart. If we think highly of or love someone, we find ourselves thinking of them often. This must be our attitude toward the instructions given by God though His word.

Qualities to possess: humility, honesty, integrity and hard work
Read Proverbs 6:1-19

You have probably heard the saying, "An idle mind is the devil's workshop." The following principles are given between the Lord's instructions on the effects of immorality and His warning against immoral living. Obviously these characteristics reflect the wisdom of God and will prevent the foolish activity that would destroy our character.

In order to be a person of your word you must carefully consider the commitments you make. Verses 1-5 instruct us to be willing to admit when we make a mistake and be quick to correct it.

The admonitions of verses 6-11 are to be industrious and energetic in our work habits—a principle repeated several times in the New Testament (Ephesians 5:28; 2 Thessalonians 3:10-13; 1 Timothy 5:8).

The wicked or worthless person is one who refuses to take a stand for righteousness. Depicted as a fraudulent person that pretends to be something he is not, the wicked person is not content with his life. His life will be plagued with trouble, and he can never see that his own rebellious disposition is the problem (vs. 12-15).

It is imperative that we learn and understand the things enumerated in verses 16-19, for they are that which God hates. As we examine these abominable conditions, let each of us humbly consider our own character.

Memorize and meditate

"Treasure my commands within you. Keep my commands and live."

- Proverbs 7:1, 2

(Take a moment to also meditate on 1 Corinthians 6:15-20)

Discuss specific behaviors associated with each of these characteristics:

- A proud look

- A lying tongue

- Hands that shed innocent blood

- A heart that devises wickedness

- Feet that run to evil

- False witness

- One who sows discord

Our future walk with God depends upon our receiving this wisdom from above. We must accept personal responsibility for our actions and deliver ourselves by avoiding laziness and identifying those things that God hates.

Wisdom will deliver us from the deception of indecency
Read Proverbs 6:20-7:27

The sexual desires we possess are not evil. The continuance of mankind is a result God's instruction to replenish the earth. However, men have corrupted the beauty of the relationship of a husband and wife by having unlawful relationships. These unlawful relationships are called adultery and fornication. Each of these are sinful and will keep us from going to heaven. But God will deliver us from these if we will receive His instructions.

Though we may not fully understand why God has ordered relationships the way He has, we can be certain His way is the way of life. Guidance from God is a lamp, a light, and the way of life (6:23). This wisdom will keep us from the deception of immorality (7:5).

Comprehending the power of the enticement to commit sexual immorality will help us to understand why God instructs us to avoid its appearance. A man is reduced to a crust of bread. All who were slain by her were strong men (6:26; 7:26).

Your commitment not to commit sexual immorality will only be as strong as your commitment to avoid circumstances that stimulate your desire. You cannot play with fire and not expect to get burned (6:27-28).

The character of people willing to commit immorality is **unstable**. They make promises they cannot keep. They refuse to accept **personal responsibility** for themselves, and their actions are an **abomination** to God.

Though they may present themselves as desiring an **innocent relationship**, they really are seeking to **destroy** your innocence and serve **themselves**.

The crafty, deceptive ways of those who would lure us into immoral living are those who consider us to be a naive person, devoid of understanding (7:7). But through the knowledge and wisdom gained in this study, we will not be taken advantage of or robbed of our innocence.

The enticing words of the immoral are set to deceive the heart of the unprepared. They promise secret pleasures but deliver sorrow upon sorrow.

Questions to consider

1. Is it wrong to be attracted to someone of the opposite sex? _____

    _____

2. How can you identify immoral people? _____

    _____

    _____

3. How are we able to avoid committing sexual immorality? _____

    _____

    _____

4. How will humility, honesty, integrity, and hard work deliver you from immoral people?

    _____

    _____

    _____

Light to Live By: The Excellent Way of Wisdom

Getting focused

Wisdom, like God, does not change. The precepts and principles of God's word are timeless. In chapters eight and nine, we discover why. Wisdom comes to life in this chapter, possessing the characteristics and attributes that are revealed as that of deity. The insight given in words of wisdom is older than time itself. Before the world was created, wisdom was there. It is this insight that should ignite and maintain our interest. The words of wisdom are truly our insight to life and living. Through wisdom and understanding we learn our purpose in life. We must identify that purpose and pursue it.

Possibly realizing the difficulty one may have in accepting the things stated in the previous study regarding immorality, God reminds us of the supreme nature of wisdom.

Instruction is our most valuable commodity
Read Proverbs 8:1-21

How much would you be willing to pay for a good book—ten, maybe twenty dollars? The wisdom imparted by the words of truth are more valuable than all earthly possessions combined. Learning to evaluate and appreciate God's word is the key to opening the door to spiritual fulfillment.

The wisdom from God is available to all. She cries out in a public way that all can hear. Both the foolish and the prudent hear. The determination of one's character is made by the value one places on her teachings.

The things God teaches us are plain, simple, and right. But not all understand or accept them. Those who find understanding will cherish them above silver, gold, or precious stones. "All the things one may desire cannot be compared with her" (v. 11).

Given the opportunity to ask for anything, Solomon asked for wisdom. The result of the request led him to become

> "Take my **instruction** and not silver, and **knowledge** rather than choicest gold."
>
> - Proverbs 8:10

the most materially blessed man who has ever lived. At a glance, we can see wisdom delivers much more than words; wisdom provides a way of life. The ability to make wise decisions is the first product of wisdom. Additionally, understanding and strength are other characteristics.

The qualities that lead to successful leadership are produced by words of instruction. They can only be found in paths of righteousness.

Wisdom speaks from experience
Read Proverbs 8:22-36

The perfect order of creation is the result of the wisdom of God. It is for this reason we are spoken to as children. The authority to instruct has been established. The only conditional element that remains for man is the desire to receive the instructions expressed by wisdom.

Mankind's search for the answers of life are found in God's revelation to man. As we grow we must listen, watch, and wait to gain understanding. In so doing, we will find the way to life—not only an elevated physical existence but also favor in the eyes of the Lord.

The word of God is alive. It is far more than a printed page, and through receiving it, we are the crown of God's creation. The gift of God is free to all men. To refuse to receive life is to rob yourself of God's goodness. You exchange life for death. Jesus said, "the words that I speak, they are Spirit and they are life" (John 6:63).

God has opened the door; go in
Read Proverbs 9:1-18

The house of God is built and furnished; we need only to move in. Verse 10 reveals the central aspect to all wisdom and the foundation of foolishness, which is your acknowledgment and respect or disregard for the Creator of all things.

Wisdom provides the keys to your future home. All the necessities for one's contented existence are made available. The invitation to come in is made. It is at this invitation that we must choose to enter in or turn away.

What is your response when someone corrects you? Do you look to return criticism? Your response will identify

"To whom you present yourselves slaves to obey, **you are that one's slave whom you obey**, whether of sin leading to death, or of obedience leading to righteousness."

- Romans 6:16

Memorize and meditate

"I love those who love me, and those who seek me diligently will find me."

- Proverbs 8:17

and determine your character. Anger rejects instruction. Patient consideration of instruction produces wisdom, justice, and love.

The opportunity to do right is likened to that of doing wrong. Both call out, we must answer. In this, we learn that the real nature of man is his ability to choose.

Questions to consider

1. Find two things that inform us what the fear of the Lord is. _____

    _____

    _____

2. What do foolishness and wisdom have in common? _____

    _____

    _____

3. How does wisdom accomplish all the things it claims in this study? _____

    _____

    _____

Ensuring Success: Wisdom's Way of Doing Business

Getting focused

God's way is the way of righteousness. The psalmist David defines righteousness in Psalms 119:172: "all your commandments are righteousness." The righteous are mentioned twenty times in our text. Simply stated, the righteous are those who listen and are obedient to God's word. The result of obtaining wisdom is righteous living. Righteousness is not merely possessing accurate information but the application of precepts and principles that produce a godly life. As we investigate those things relative to the righteous, let us consider a practical manner in which we may employ them in our lives.

The forthcoming lessons contain an incredible amount of information. We will not be able to address each precept but only highlight various thoughts within the text. Make notes of particular passages you find helpful and informative, and we will discuss them during our study period.

Dedicated commitment with an everlasting foundation

Read Proverbs 10

"Blessed are those who hunger and thirst for righteousness, for they shall be filled" (Matthew 5:6). The first step in our pursuit of happiness must be the desire to do what is right. The spiritual blessings received from God begin with our diligent attitude.

Terms such as "the hand of the diligent" (v. 4), "the labor" (v. 16), and "the desire" (v. 24) are associated with those who receive strength from the Lord. The promise that the Lord will not allow the righteous soul to famish is founded upon an industrious spirit (v. 3). This quality is critical in our walk with God. The apostle Paul encourages us to not grow weary while doing good, for in due season we shall reap if we do not lose heart (Galatians 6:9).

7 Pillars of Wisdom

1. Ethics

2. Humility

3. Instruction

4. Discipline

5. Knowledge

6. Integrity

7. Honesty

A clear contrast between two roads in life is drawn in chapter ten: one road is identified as the way of righteousness, the other is the way of the wicked. Below we have listed the distinction. Which road are you traveling?

	The Way of Righteousness	The Way of the Wicked
Verse 3	Provision	Starvation
Verse 16	Life	(Death) Sin
Verse 21	Abundance	Emptiness
Verse 24	Confidence	Fear
Verse 25	Eternal	Temporal
Verse 28	Gladness	Bleakness
Verse 30	Stability	Destitute
Verse 32	Knowledge	Ignorant

Qualities that ensure success: grace, mercy, and generosity
Read Proverbs 11

The way we interact with others has much to do with our future happiness and success. God promises prosperity. However, this prosperity is not accidental but calculated and premeditated. He who sows righteousness has a sure reward (v. 18b).

Integrity is defined as a steadfast adherence to a strict moral or ethical code (American Heritage Dictionary). This quality enables us to remain focused on our purpose and future. Because of this, our decisions are based upon truth, and we are trusted by those with whom we come in contact.

These characteristics begin with humility (v. 2). Humility is that quality that allows God to guide you. This results in fruits of the Spirit, which are love, joy, peace, longsuffering, kindness, goodness, faithfulness, gentleness and self-control (Galatians 5:22-23).

True success is measured in honesty and uprightness. Though dishonesty can bring monetary gain, it leads to poverty (v. 24). But those who are concerned about the welfare of others become rich. Success is not measured by the size of your bank account or the number of your possessions.

"There is one who **scatters**, and yet **increases all the more**, and there is one who **withholds** what is justly due, and yet it results only in **want**."

- Proverbs 11:24

Success is assured for:

- A gracious woman (v. 16)
- A merciful man (v. 17)
- The generous soul (v. 25)

There are many things that we may endeavor to gain in this life, but the fruit of righteousness is a tree of life, and he who wins souls is wise (v. 30).

Diligence is man's precious possession
Read Proverbs 12; note verse 27b

As we stress the right way to engage in business, note the continued contrast between being industrious and being lazy. Righteousness, wisdom, and prosperity are not a matter of luck, but exercise of effort, will, and ability.

The key to enjoying the fruit of our labor is enjoying work. "He who tills the land is satisfied with bread" (v. 11). Joy and happiness are realized when we learn contentment (Ecclesiastes 9:9, 10). "Godliness with contentment is great gain...and having food and clothing, with these we shall be content" (1 Timothy 6:6-8).

Four important points need to emphasized and adopted from this chapter:

1. Love instruction (v. 1)
2. Do not follow frivolity (v. 11)
3. Be satisfied with good (v. 14)
4. Choose your friends carefully (v. 26)

The real distinction between foolishness and wisdom is found in our attitude toward service. The hand of the diligent will rule, but the lazy man will be put to forced labor (v. 24). Diligence and laziness are both founded upon attitudes which translate into activity.

The despicable state of the lazy leads to discontent, while those who have a mind to work find contentment, joy, and blessing.

Identifying and obtaining true wealth
Read Proverbs 13

A key maxim in unlocking the treasure of true wealth is found in the comprehension of two verses. "The soul of the lazy man desires and has nothing, but the soul of

Memorize and meditate

"Anxiety in the heart of man causes depression, but a good word makes it glad."

- Proverbs 12:25

the diligent shall be made rich" (v. 4). "There is one who makes himself rich, yet has nothing; and one who makes himself poor, yet has great riches" (v. 7).

Our pursuit of prosperity must be accompanied by instruction in righteousness. If all we obtain through our endeavors in life is an abundance of possessions, we have nothing. If we are destitute of material possessions but have fellowship with God, we are rich.

The apostle Paul expressed his ability to find happiness regardless of his financial circumstances (Philippians 4:12, 13). In Christ, even in poverty we are rich (Revelation 2:9-10). Examine in contrast Revelation 3:17. What determines wealth?

Prosperity, happiness, and contentment are states of mind that are produced by a heart that "hungers and thirsts after righteousness, for they shall be filled" (Matthew 5:6). In contrast, "those who desire to be rich fall into temptation and a snare and into many foolish and harmful lusts which drown men in destruction and perdition...and pierce themselves through with many sorrows" (1 Timothy 6:9, 10).

The vault in which true wealth is secure is the heart of faith. Valuables kept in any other place are an easy target for the thief (John 10:10).

Questions to consider

1. Examine and discuss the following passages concerning the importance of developing the ability and proper manner in which we communicate with others.

    a. Proverbs 10:11 _____

    _____

    b. Proverbs 11:9, 11 _____

    _____

    c. Proverbs 12:13, 17-22 _____

    _____

2. Why is diligence your precious possession (12:27)? _____

    _____

    _____

3. What is the result of diligently seeking righteousness?_____

    _____

    _____

Introspection: The Wise Heart Knows Itself

Getting focused

Our previous study led us to three qualities we must possess in order to obtain the true riches of wisdom: dedication, diligence, and discernment. As we continue to allow God to lead us in the path of righteousness, we must learn yet another characteristic of truth, wisdom, and righteousness: the conscience. A term often used in Scripture to identify conscience is the heart. An activity of the conscience is to think. Within this chapter we find the frequently quoted verse, "There is a way that seems right to a man, but the end is the way of death" (14:12).

One of the single most important elements in living the Christian life is being honest with yourself. The previous lesson taught us that being honest with others is the right way to do business. In this lesson we will be introduced to the conscience. The conscience is the element within your heart that considers good and bad and will either excuse or condemn thoughts and intentions. To be deceived by worldliness is to allow our conscience to be hardened against the truth. The result of deception will lead us into spiritual blindness.

An open mind finds wisdom
Read Proverbs 14:1-9

The scoffer of verse 6 is one who despises authority. Such a one may seek wisdom but will never find it. Herein lies the difference between a future filled with spiritual blessings from God and a life filled with the bitterness of the world.

The attitude of one that rejects authority is contagious. Thus, we are instructed to avoid contact with such men (v. 7). We are to identify those who reject authority by listening to what they say. Fools mock at sin (v. 9). You can know those whom you must avoid by their attitude toward sin.

Friends, music, and entertainment that make light of sin lead us in the way of vain pride, confusion, and deceit.

"**Leave** the presence of a fool, or you **will not discern** words of knowledge."

- Proverbs 14:7

The volatility of the conscience
Read Proverbs 14:10-14

The conscience can condemn or approve anything you do. Self-awareness of guilt resides in the conscience. Though one may deceive himself or cover up his true feelings, the heart knows its own bitterness (v. 10).

The convicting element of the conscience can bring bitterness or joy. The reality of either is realized in the response to guilt. We can excuse ourselves by self-justification or be satisfied from above (v. 14).

The failure to respond properly to our conscience will produce:

- Bitterness (v. 10)

- Spiritual death (v. 12)

- Sorrow and grief (v. 13)

A deceptive avenue through which worldliness lures us is laughter and what appears to a good time—both of which are superfluous expressions that mask the hardened heart. In the quiet moments separated from pseudo-happiness, we find true sorrow and grief (v. 13).

The danger of backsliding is losing sight of reality and allowing sinful, destructive behavior to become an acceptable way of life (v. 14). We must ever acknowledge that God is greater than our heart and knows all things (1 John 3:20).

The walk of the wise looks carefully where he steps
Read Proverbs 14:15-25

Honest self-examination in light of God's inspired revelation is the only method for knowing one's conscience. The only proper response is to depart from evil (v. 16).

However, a common response to guilt is anger and denial. Our only release from such foolish deception is mercy and truth. Mercy and truth belong to those who devise good (v. 22).

Good intentions lay the foundation for knowledge, understanding, wisdom, and happiness. One rich in character is also rich in relationships. The kind of relationships you have with others will give you insight to properly see yourself.

Memorize and meditate

"There is a way that seems right to a man, but its end is the way of death."

- Proverbs 14:12

Oppression, anger, and envy: a reproach to any people

Read Proverbs 14:26-35

To be in control of your emotions is to be in control of your body, soul, and spirit.

The essence of religion is a benevolent disposition and control over our desires (James 1:26-27). All of these are revealed in our actions toward others.

A healthy spiritual heart is produced by proper respect and reverence for God. The result is a form of confidence that has no place for anger or envy. Anger and envy are produced when one lacks understanding. G. K. Chesterton wrote, "Bigotry may be roughly defined as the anger of men who have no opinions."

Questions to consider

1. What two elements are essential in gaining understanding (vs. 6b, 29)? _____

    _____

    _____

2. Discuss how we identify being filled with our own ways as opposed to being satisfied

    from above. _____

    _____

    _____

3. Read and discuss Philippians 4:6-7, 11-13. _____

    _____

    _____

The Mirror of Our Heart: The Words We Speak

Getting focused

One of the most difficult things we are called to do is to control what we say. The overall purpose of this study is to gain insight into those things that are right before we do those that are wrong. The control of the tongue begins with the preparation of the heart. Our words reflect what is in our heart. "For out of the heart the mouth speaks." To control what we say, we must control what we think. To control what we think, we must control what we put into our minds. The power and logic of this study will aid us in our every endeavor. The great task of controlling what we say can only be accomplished through the assimilation of the wisdom that comes from God.

Proper disposition and doctrine make the difference
Read Proverbs 15

We must learn to approach every situation with the proper temperament. The result in doing this will turn difficult confrontations into profitable discussions. Verses 1 and 2 inform us that it is not sufficient to merely possess knowledge, but we must also be able to express it in a proper manner.

If we find our relationships with others burdened by constant argument, we need to examine and alter our manner of communication. Proper communication brings:

- A cheerful countenance (v. 13)

- Calms contentions (v. 18)

- Joyful living (v. 23)

Other elements necessary in our communication with others are truth and righteousness. The basis for all truth is founded upon God's word. Therefore, before we can effectively communicate we must study. The first requirement in proper communication is listening (v. 5).

> "The tongue of the **wise** makes knowledge **acceptable**, but the mouth of **fools** spouts **folly**."
>
> - Proverbs 15:2

The second is thinking, and thirdly, speaking (v. 28). Too often we speak before we think. This leads us to say many foolish, damaging things that bring regret and grief.

Throughout this chapter you will notice the relationship of those who are willing to listen and learn with those who are righteous and wise (vs. 31-33). "The heart of the righteous studies how he will answer" (v. 28).

A modern day proverb states, "It is better to remain silent and allow others to think you are ignorant, than to open your mouth and remove all doubt."

A submissive mind leads to the control of the tongue
Read Proverbs 16

When we willingly allow God to guide and direct our steps, His controlling influence permeates every area of our lives. For those committed to Christ, even your thoughts shall be established (v. 3).

Notice the manner in which God operates in the life of the righteous:

- We prepare the heart to receive instruction; God provides the words of instruction (v. 1).

- We commit our actions to things right; God establishes our thoughts (v. 3).

- When we please God, God provides peace (v. 7).

- We plan our lives around God; God directs our steps (v. 9).

The passages mark the path that leads to wisdom and righteousness. It begins with your desire, dedication, and acceptance of God's word, but it depends upon God's grace, truth, and mercy (v. 6). To possess this spirit and learn this principle is to find true happiness (v. 20).

The single element that prevents one from receiving direction and blessings from God is **pride**! We must recognize our heart to be the fountain through which blessings flow or the source from which trouble, strife, and separation from God come. Pride is the contemptuous, arrogant attitude that can rise up within a person when they are given instruction and correction. Humility is that state in which God exalts us (1 Peter 5:6).

Memorize and meditate

"Pride goes before destruction and a haughty spirit before a fall."

- Proverbs 16:8

Jesus said, "What comes out of a man, that defiles a man. For from within, out of the heart, proceed evil thoughts, adulteries, fornication...pride..." (Mark 7:20-22).

Though we often say things we should not, desire accompanied by wisdom eliminates careless speech. "The heart of the wise teaches his mouth, and adds learning to his lips" (v. 23).

Questions to consider

1. How should we respond to someone who is angry with us?_____

   _____

   _____

2. What is the best method to use in making plans for the future (15:22)?_____

   _____

   _____

3. What do a positive attitude, pleasant words, and a heart that trusts in God have in

   common (15:13, 26; 16:20)? _____

   _____

   _____

Seeking Love: Tests of True Friendship

Getting focused

Forming wholesome relationships requires the proper application of wisdom. Critical to receiving the spiritual blessings and benefits from God is our attitude and actions toward others.

The peace of God can only come to those who strive to have peace with mankind. These relationships come by our exercising discretion in whom we choose to confide. Rebellion brings grief, shame, and eventual destruction. The source of this trouble is selfishness.

Proper relationships are formed by those who seek love
Read Proverbs 17

When we display a pleasant, benevolent, sincere personality we produce wonderful relationships. The principles revealed in this text are universal. Verse 9 expresses the foundation for all relationships: seek love. Love is not something we find in a place but is a thing created by effort and desire. We must understand, love is a choice of action, not merely an emotional response.

The Lord examines the heart (v. 3). His word makes known the manner in which He views us. The test of friendship is not in words but in actions (1 John 3:17-18).

How do you respond to:

- Lies and unkind things said about others (v. 4)?

- News of tragedy or trouble experienced by others (v. 5)?

- The mistakes and shortcomings of others (v. 9; Matthew 18)?

- Someone correcting you (vs. 10-11)?

If you constantly find fault with others but see nothing wrong with yourself, you probably have been deceived (v. 20). In contrast, one who has a positive outlook and seeks to bring

"But whoever has the world's goods, and sees his brother in **need** and **closes his heart** against him, how does the **love of God** abide in him? Little children, let us not love with word or with tongue, but in **deed and truth**."

- 1 John 3:17-18

"He who **restrains** his words has **knowledge**, and he who has a cool spirit is a man of understanding. Even a **fool**, when he keeps **silent**, is **considered wise**; when he closes his lips, he is considered prudent."

- Proverbs 17:27-28

the best out of others brings happiness to himself, as well as to others (v. 22).

Friendship qualities are developed by:

- Resolving problems before they start (v. 14)

- Keeping a secret (v. 9)

- Being loyal in times of trouble (v. 9, 17)

Two critical aspects in all relationships are maintaining a calm disposition at all times, and thinking things through before you say them (vs. 27-28).

So many friendships are destroyed by unkind words. The illustration of strife being like releasing water can appropriately be applied to the words we speak. Once they are released we cannot put them back.

Self-centered conversation is a reproach to one's character
Read Proverbs 18

As we seek positive relationships and interactions with others, we must first develop the character, temperament, and personality of one who is concerned about others. Isolation is a sign of selfishness. Though we are not to associate with the worldly, we are to show ourselves as people of honor and integrity.

A fundamental quality of being a friend is listening with an understanding ear. Much of our future will be molded by the manner in which we listen.

Verse 1 identifies one's negative response to the wisdom expressed by others. Aggravation and isolation are not appropriate responses. Even at difficult levels of communication, the wise listens to all one has to say before rendering an opinion. "He who answers a matter before he hears it, it is folly and shame to him" (v. 13).

A sure road to loneliness is to be quick to express yourself but slow to listen. The "know it all" will find himself viewed by others with contempt and criticism (v. 3), which results in contention (v. 6). The problem of being quick to speak not only interferes with earthly relationships, but his lips are the snare of his soul (v. 7).

Our personal outlook has a substantial effect on our ability to cope with difficulty (v. 14). Whether it be physical infirmity or corrupt people in power, a positive attitude carries many benefits. The principles expressed in vs. 16-23 are considerations for effective communication.

- A practical application of effective communication is to express appreciation for an anticipated desirable response (v. 16).

- Be prepared for a rebuttal when stating your side of some occurrence (v. 17).

- Sometimes the best method of settling a matter is to flip a coin (v. 18).

- Saying the wrong thing can create a wall of resistance (v. 19).

- The art of persuasion is the best approach for the underdog (v. 23).

- To find a life long companion is a good thing (v. 22)!

Fair weather friends will fail us
Read Proverbs 19

Those who befriend us because of material possessions are not true friends. Those kinds of friends will only be there for us as long as we have something they need or want. This chapter explains how it is better to be lonely and have character than to seek relationships with the worldly. Integrity can cause one to suffer loneliness.

Patience in choosing friends is very important to our spiritual future. Though we are to possess a generous spirit, we must exercise discretion so others do not take advantage of us.

There is a clear distinction between those who lack possessions because of moral integrity and those who are poor due to laziness. Laziness is characteristic of one who fails to properly reverence God (compare vs. 15 and 24 with 23).

Wisdom is to be applied to every relationship. We must recognize the relationships established and provided for us by God are to be revered and cherished.

Memorize and meditate

"A man who has friends must himself be friendly, but there is a friend who sticks closer than a brother."

- Proverbs 18:24

- Parents should view their children as God's gift and a keen sense of responsibility must follow (v. 18). A relationship that must not fail (22:6).

- Children should honor and reverence their parents. These relationships are formed through listening (vs. 26, 27).

- Husbands must view their wives as a provision from God (v. 14b).

- Friendship: "Two are better than one, because they have a good reward for their labor. For if they fall, one will lift up his companion. But woe to him who is alone when he falls, for he has no one to help him up...Though one be overpowered by another, two can withstand him. And a threefold cord is not quickly broken" (Ecclesiastes 4:9-12).

Questions to consider

1. Make a practical application of Proverbs 17:13. _____

_____

_____

2. Identify at least two aspects of being a good friend. _____

_____

_____

3. How is a merry heart like medicine (17:22), and how does the spirit of a man sustain

him in sickness (18:14a)? _____

_____

_____

Obstruction to Wisdom: A Lack of Discipline

Getting focused

As we have examined in earlier studies, wisdom is the proper application of knowledge. However, there are many things that obscure our view of what truth truly is. Because they distort knowledge, these perversions obstruct our ability to apply wisdom in our lives. In fact, many of these prevent us from being able to discern even simple truth. The deceitful nature of certain activities bring about spiritual blindness. However, "the spirit of a man is the lamp of the Lord, searching all the inner depths of his heart" (20:27). God's word is the mirror of our soul. If we will look into it and obey it, we can know the truth and walk in wisdom (James 1:23-27).

The things that obstruct our ability to apply the righteous principles taught in God's word are impatience, pride, materialism, and intoxication. Each of these grow out of a lack of discipline.

Sobriety today makes for a brighter tomorrow
Read Proverbs 20

"Listen to counsel and receive instruction, that you may be wise in your latter days" (19:20). Several things are noteworthy in this chapter which, if accepted, will guide us through our formative years.

Verse one introduces us to one of the most deceitful, damaging, obstructors of wisdom—intoxicants. All mind-altering drugs may be included in our assessment, because each lead us astray. Other related characteristics of being "under the influence" that dim our view of the future are:

- Laziness (vs. 4, 13)

- Lying (v. 19)

- Impatience (vs. 21, 22)

- Dishonesty (v. 23)

"The **sluggard** does not plow after the autumn, so he **begs** during the harvest and **has nothing**."

- Proverbs 20:4

Remorse is all that is left at the end of unwise activity. The allurements of this world, at first, delight our senses, but the result is empty bitterness. It is this emptiness within that leads to further darkness. All the "get rich quick" schemes and preparations for momentary pleasures fail. Impatience breeds foolishness and robs us of life's richest blessings (v. 21).

If we willingly apply the knowledge received from the Lord, we will receive strength in our youth and glory in our old age (v. 29).

Contentment, moderation, and planning today lead to a prosperous tomorrow
Read Proverbs 21 and 22

Money has its value. However, we must make proper application of our resources to gain any benefit from it. Extravagance leads to poverty. Laziness and selfishness are at the heart of discontent and poverty. Proper planning is the key to happiness and prosperity. The critical lesson in wisdom is to **plan for the future**. "The plans of the diligent lead surely to plenty, but those of everyone who is hasty, surely to poverty" (v. 5).

Isaiah 55:2 says, "Why spend money on what is not bread, and your labor on what does not satisfy?" Many of the material things that appeal to us do not provide any lasting joy or happiness. So, considering what we will do with our resources, we must first establish worth and priority.

> "The exercise of justice is **joy** for the righteous, but is **terror** to the workers of iniquity."
>
> - Proverbs 21:15

First, we must only derive pleasure from things honorable and righteous (v. 15). Pleasure is realized when we fulfill the desires of our heart. Desires are determined by the things that intrigue us. Though we may be inclined to prefer one thing over another, the purpose of heart is determined by knowledge and choice. If we make our plans for the future with the wise counsel of God's word, satisfaction will be derived from righteous living. "He who follows righteousness and mercy finds life, righteousness and honor" (v. 21).

Secondly, generosity holds the key to wealth. A foolish man squanders his treasure (v. 20). He who has a generous eye will be blessed (22:9). To neglect the needy is to rob oneself (v. 13).

The last step in establishing proper value and worth is humility. Humility enables us to find contentment regardless of our financial situation (Philippians 4:11-13). Humility and the fear of the Lord are riches and honor and life (22:4).

Arrogance obstructs the way of righteousness and refuses to allow the Lord to deliver us from evil (vs. 16, 26, 31).

Verses 6 and 13 of chapter 22 provide insight into a fundamental principle in learning. Discipline serves as an instrument of education when properly applied. Discipline is administered incrementally. It begins with instruction and reasoning. If these are not received, more stern measures are applied. The severity of the discipline we receive is commensurate with our response to instruction. Discipline is not a pleasant experience, but the result is the peaceable fruit of righteousness (Hebrews 12:5-12). Though discipline can be painful, it will deliver our soul from hell (23:13).

Many things deceive; consider carefully what is before you
Read Proverbs 23

"Buy the truth and sell it not" (v. 23) is an admonition we must always carry with us. When we obtain the truth, we must be careful not to sell it for things of lesser value, and nothing is more valuable than the truth. Several of the things addressed in this chapter are those that deceivingly present themselves as having greater value than simple truth.

Our motives, as well as the motives of others, must always be challenged. The worldly seek self-gratification even at the expense of their soul. The allurement of the finer things in life often expose us to be used and abused by others. When we are overly motivated for this world's possessions, disappointment is certain (vs. 1-9).

Jesus asks, "For what profit is it to a man if he gains the whole world, and lose his own soul? Or what shall a man give in exchange for his soul?" (Matthew 16:26)

It is imperative to recognize the seductive nature of worldliness before you are exposed to it. For parents, this instruction must be clear and forceful. The extremities of discipline are usually not understood by the one to whom it is administered, however, the end result is deliverance of the soul from harm (vs. 10-28).

There are two things briefly addressed that inhibit spiritual growth and rob us of truth: sobriety, or the lack thereof (vs. 20-21), and immorality (vs. 26-28).

Memorize and meditate

"He who follows righteousness and mercy finds life, righteousness and honor."

- Proverbs 21:21

These are the two critical issues facing young men and women, and they often go together. The first step in avoiding both is not to mix with those who are willing to engage in such activity (1 Corinthians 6:9-10; 2 Corinthians 6:14-16).

The addictive, destructive nature of alcohol is vividly described in vs. 29-35. Compare this with the glamorization depicted in the media today. These words from God detail the result of those who give in to the pressure to participate in drinking or taking drugs. The majority of crime, many of the deaths due to traffic accidents, and numerous birth defects in newborns all stem from the use of drugs and alcohol. These destroy ones ability to reason; thus, to participate in these, you have sold the truth and moved the ancient landmark (vs. 10, 23).

Not only are drugs and alcohol responsible for many social ills, but those who do these things forfeit eternal life. The appeal of these at first seem to serve as a means of having a good time, yet the end result is that one becomes enslaved by them (v. 35).

Questions to consider

1. Name three things that are necessary to ensure a financially stable future. _____

   _____

   _____

2. Drugs and alcohol being so destructive, why do you suppose so many people use

   them? _____

   _____

   _____

Lesson 12

Enlightened Through Observation: Viewing Others in the Proper Perspective

Getting focused

We find simple principles reiterated in this chapter. It has been said that three principles in teaching are repeat, repeat, repeat. The fundamental element which will ensure our prosperity is our heart's desire. These desires must be molded through careful consideration of what God desires of us. This attitude is easy to develop when we realize that, "for a righteous man may fall seven times and rise again, but the wicked shall fall by calamity" (24:16).

Three fundamental essentials for spiritual shelter: wisdom, understanding, and knowledge
Read Proverbs 24:1-10

Building a life for oneself involves developing relationships. Our perception of what is "cool" forms our opinions and pursuits. When we are attracted to the company of those who reject godly activity, we take our first step toward foolish behavior. We may find ourselves intrigued by the immoral activity of acquaintances, but if we allow this to develop into a relationship (fellowship) our spiritual strength will fail.

Home ownership has long been considered the "American dream." Verses 3 and 4 use this analogy to increase our desire for righteous things. Our shelter from the world is built, established, and furnished in the ways of righteousness. Those devoid of this truth can only pursue the possessions of others, for they have no sense to obtain them themselves. Those who constantly attempt to make themselves feel better by degrading others are contemptible.

How to respond to your uninformed friends
Read Proverbs 24:11-20

Our actions and reactions to those with whom we come in contact speak volumes about our character. Knowledge and wisdom are not limited to personal applications but must be

"Through **wisdom** a house is **built**, and by understanding it is established; by **knowledge** the rooms are filled with all **precious and pleasant riches**."

- Proverbs 24:3-4

shared and demonstrated before those who do not know truth. Verse 11 implies we ought not rush to judgment toward those who are without God. Additionally, verses 17 and 18 instruct us to avoid a vengeful spirit. "Beloved do not avenge yourselves, but rather give place to wrath; for it is written, 'Vengeance is Mine, I will repay,' says the Lord. Therefore, 'If your enemy is hungry, feed him; if he is thirsty, give him drink; for in so doing you will heap coals of fire on his head.' Do not be overcome with evil, but overcome evil with good" (Romans 12:19-21).

One of the most influential characteristics of Christianity is the positive view of the future. This optimistic outlook is based upon the joy that knowledge delivers to your soul and the assurance that the ultimate end of your life is heaven. The number seven in Scripture often represents completeness or the totality of a thing. The message of verse 16 is that we shall rise above every adversity and trial. The doom of the wicked is certain. Though they may seem to prosper for the moment, "there will be no future for the evil man; the lamp of the wicked will be put out" (v. 20).

Reprove error, respect all men, and honor those in positions of authority
Read Proverbs 24:21-29

A real problem in our formative years of adulthood is allowing prejudice to creep in and distort our perception of others. Right and wrong must be determined by absolute principles and not be relative to the individual involved. It is easy to excuse sinful behavior of friends while pointing out the flaws of our enemies.

Those "given to change" (v. 21) refers to those who rebel against the powers that be. Honor must be given to civil rule that does not interfere with service to God. Acts 17:26-27 explains why we are to respect the governing authority. Also, this command is elaborated upon in Romans 13:1-7.

We must love all men. "Let love be without hypocrisy" (Romans 12:9). Prejudicial judgment will lead to our own condemnation (Matthew 7:1, 2). This does not mean no judgment is to be made, but we must make righteous judgments. "Those who rebuke the wicked will have delight, and a good blessing will come upon them" (v. 25).

Memorize and meditate

"Those who rebuke the wicked will have delight, and a good blessing shall come upon them."

- Proverbs 24:25

Wisdom also comes through observation

Read Proverbs 24:30-34

Little can be added to the illustration of this text. The main point we would like to observe is that knowledge was imparted in this manner: "I looked on it and received instruction" (v. 32).

We can be assured of the destination of laziness without going there. Remember one purpose of this study is to know the result of wrong decisions before we make them. Observing the foolishness of others is a pathway to wisdom.

Questions to consider

1. Describe the various ways we may judge others. _____

   _____

   _____

2. Why, or in what way, do those who rebuke the wicked "delight?" _____

   _____

   _____

Behavior Management: Demonstrating Wisdom

Getting focused

Wisdom is something that must be demonstrated. Though knowledge will enable one to answer questions correctly, wisdom will empower you to act and react properly to the various circumstances of life. The situations portrayed in these chapters, though written centuries ago, are as relevant as if they were written yesterday. Acceptance and application of these precepts will help you to make the right decisions in every area of your life.

Exercise humility and patience when approaching governing authorities
Read Proverbs 25:1-15

Central to the first 15 verses of this chapter are instructions on the proper disposition we are to possess before those who are in positions of political power. These precepts are universal in nature and should become characteristics of our character.

A distinction is made between an earthly ruler and our heavenly Father. Leaders are not to attempt to consider themselves as "gods" but are to investigate and identify righteousness. Verses 4 and 5 identify how a righteous government is established. The corrupt governments of our culture demonstrate the relationship between wicked men and the unrighteous kingdoms of the world.

Humility before those who are in positions of authority is a more effective way of obtaining their favor than aggressive or arrogant behavior (vs. 6-7). Also, the risk of putting yourself in an embarrassing situation is diminished. Patience must be exercised to sway the minds of those in power. Verse 15 illustrates the force that patient forbearance and restraint of the tongue has over physical brawn.

Self-control must be exercised in dealing with our fellow citizens. Verses 8 through 10 are specific instructions for

> "Do not **exalt yourself** in the presence of the **king**, and do not stand in the place of the great."
>
> - Proverbs 25:6

interaction between friends and neighbors. The primary prevailing element that should govern all relationships is a willingness to communicate. Jesus offers a specific directive in Matthew 18:15-17 for a Christian to communicate to a fellow Christian who has sinned. Sadly, this is one of the most frequently violated commands of God.

Memorize and meditate

"Whoever has no rule over his own spirit is like a city broken down without walls."

- Proverbs 25:28

Exercise caution when selecting relationships

Read Proverbs 25:16-28

Before one can build relationships with others he must be in control of his own life. Verse 28 can be associated with all the preceding admonitions and instructions that pertain to our lives with others. "Whoever has no rule over his own spirit is like a city broken down, without walls." If we can not control our own lives, we can do little to have a positive influence on others.

Have you ever eaten too many sweets? Though delicious while being eaten, after a time they make you sick (v. 16). Too much of a good thing is not good. The idea of self-control is conveyed in the statement, "eat only as much as you need." Moderation and self-control must permeate every thing we do.

"Don't wear out your welcome." We must be careful not to overextend ourselves in relationships that don't demand it (v. 17). In contrast, verse 25 describes the refreshing nature of a timely visit and words of encouragement.

Great discretion must be utilized prior to our placing trust or confidence in others. Relying on the unreliable can be devastating and painful. Verses 18-19 speak plainly about the pain that will be inflicted on the unsuspecting victim of false or unfaithful friends.

Additionally, an untimely or inappropriate response will do more harm than good. It is important to learn how to respond properly to specific situations. We ought to never allow those who consider themselves to be our enemies to alter our kind disposition (v. 22). Romans 12:19-21 repeats this proverb and adds that appropriate activity is the method by which we overcome evil with good. This text corresponds with verse 26 that speaks of the righteous man's failure to maintain his integrity before the wicked.

Identify and beware of foolish, lazy, and contentious people

Read Proverbs 26

Much of our behavior is controlled by the influence of others. It is imperative that we identify certain types of individuals and prepare for our interactions with them. Take note of the thought in the first two verses: do not bestow honor on the undeserving, and do not be affected by unjust criticism or off-handed remarks of others.

We must never lower ourselves to the same level as the foolish. We lend credence to foolishness by either participating in their foolish behavior or acting as if their foolishness is entertaining—i.e. listening to or laughing at their jokes or gestures (vs. 4-5).

We are inviting trouble when we place our trust or confidence in the undeserving. A test to determine who qualifies as foolish is one who repeatedly acts foolish (v. 11).

Even more despicable than a fool is one who is vain. This person is beyond the reach of reason and learning, perceiving themselves to know everything (v. 12).

The lazy individual is one who demonstrates a quality beyond foolishness (vs. 13-16).

The contentious person has many of the same characteristics of the foolish. However, their behavior is more extreme. Not content with silliness or repeated acts of ignorance, the contentious person premeditates deceit and intentionally tells things that harm others.

Because the intentions of the impure are disguised by the use of flattery, they are difficult to identify. We must be watchful of those who continuously speak things in a joking manner or always have something negative to say about others (vs. 18-20). An individual that intends to harm another usually does not broadcast his intentions but hides them until an opportune time to inflict the most damage.

An important lesson in this study is honesty with others and oneself. Ultimately the heart of an individual will be made known (v. 26).

"Do you see a man **wise in his own eyes**? There is more hope for a fool than for him."

- Proverbs 26:12

Questions to consider

1. Name two qualities we must possess in dealing with governmental authorities.

    _____

    _____

2. What is the primary element that should govern all relationships?_____

    _____

    _____

3. Make a practical application of 25:17. _____

    _____

    _____

4. What happens when no one repeats a story they heard about another? _____

    _____

    _____

5. What lesson did you learn from 26:17? _____

    _____

    _____

Developing Disposition: Acquiring Desirable Personality Traits

Getting focused

Your personality is defined by the totality of qualities and traits which are uniquely yours. It is determined by the distinctive qualities and characteristics you demonstrate consistently by your temperamental, emotional, and mental disposition. Wisdom is not realized by introspection but perceived through personality traits which demonstrate the principles taught in God's word.

The forthcoming chapters illuminate characteristics that each of us ought to possess: reserved, yet bold; confident, but controlled. As we draw near the end of this book of wisdom we will note some of the preceding instructions are repeated for emphasis. However, in this lesson we will attempt to apply certain traits to our personality. In so doing we will obtain our goal of perceiving the words of wisdom, recognizing the obstacles and pitfalls that would do us harm. Having our hearts filled with confidence, vision, and courage, we are blessed of God and become a blessing to others. "Happy is the man who is always reverent" (28:14).

A great maxim will introduce this study which is critical to true godly wisdom: "Do not boast about tomorrow, for you do not know what a day may bring forth" (27:1). Assimilation of this single precept will remove the most undesirable personality trait known to man—vain pride.

Know your place, speak your piece, and plan with purpose
Read Proverbs 27

Let us draw three significant points from this chapter that are relevant to what constitutes our personality.

1. Developing and maintaining the proper environment to reflect the kind of person we are or desire to be (v. 8)

2. Having proper communication skills to produce a positive effect on those with whom we come in contact (v. 17)

> "As iron **sharpens** iron, so a man sharpens the **countenance** of his friend."
>
> - Proverbs 27:17

3. Making provisions for those whom you are responsible (vs. 23, 27)

Identifying certain negative traits revealed in this text will help us to avoid them. It is important to realize that though we may possess several positive characteristics, one negative quality can effect our whole persona.

- Do not be a braggart (v. 2).

- Do not conceal things that deeply effect you (v. 5).

- Do not be gullible (vs. 12-13).

- Do not be loud, obnoxious, or argumentative (vs. 14-15).

Listening to what others have to say will enable us to learn much about ourselves. Though we may perceive criticism to be unjustified, it is important to analyze the perceptions of others and examine ourselves in light of them (vs. 19, 21).

The distinguished personality of the righteous
Read Proverbs 28

All have the desire to be right. Many determine right by means of self-justification. The standard of divine righteousness is absolute and flawless. It brings joy, happiness, and peace of mind. The result of making application of the precepts of God produces a multitude of desirable personality traits.

It is imperative that the foundation for developing our personality traits begins with hearing the law (v. 9). Though we may possess a "prayerful" disposition, if we fail to listen and respond to God's word we are reprehensible. In contrast, those who open their hearts to divine instruction acquire:

- Confidence in oneself and courage to face the future (vs. 1-2)

- Perceptive insight, enabling one to make correct decisions in life—the essence of wisdom (v. 5)

- Strength to acknowledge and overcome transgressions (vs. 13, 26)

- Impartiality and the ability to judge the character of others (v. 21)

- Generosity and a benevolent disposition that is a blessing to others (v. 27)

Memorize and meditate

"A man is valued by what others say of him."

- Proverbs 27:21b

The effect of your positive personality on others

Read Proverbs 29

To possess desirable personality traits magnifies our ability to positively affect the lives of others. It must be noted that our effectiveness is contingent upon our living in accordance with God's will. Also, verses 1 and 15 explain that the development of this personality is not without difficult instruction.

One of the greatest gifts of wisdom is the ability to touch the lives of others in a positive manner. So beautifully illustrated in this chapter is the result produced by the influence of the righteous. The people rejoice (v. 2); the righteous sings and rejoices (v. 6).

In righteousness there is:

- Stability and victory over evil (vs. 14, 16)

- Happiness (v. 18)

- Honor (v. 23)

- Security (v. 25)

It is important to realize that though we have become the kind of person God would have us to be, we will not be liked by every one. There are those who oppose good. To them, you are deplorable (v. 27). Recognize there are two elements that exist in opposition to one another: good against evil, the upright against the unjust, truth against error. When we stand in the wisdom of God, the foolishness of man will oppose us.

Questions to consider

1. Why is an open rebuke better than concealed love (27:5)? _____

   _____

   _____

2. How can one's prayer be an abomination? _____

   _____

   _____

3. Name three desirable personality traits we need to acquire. _____

   _____

   _____

   _____

Illuminating Our World: Absolutes From God in the Observations of Man

Getting focused

Perception is an individual's reality. Critical to living in the light of the wisdom of God is recognizing its comprehensive nature. The word of God is to viewed as absolute and worthy of our trust. In order to receive the full benefit of God's wisdom we cannot wander beyond the confines of its enlightenment. "Every word of God is pure; He is a shield to those who put their trust in Him. Do not add to His word lest He rebuke you, and you be found a liar" (vs. 5-6).

Clear and concise principles of God may be established through observing events in nature. The verses which introduce the words of Agur, of whom we know little, establish a definitive contrast between the wisest of men when compared to the wisdom and the omniscience of God (vs. 2-4). Humility and removal of preconceived notions are essential in preparing the mind to be filled with the knowledge of God.

Two things to ask of God: truth and contentment

Read Proverbs 30:7-10

What do we want from God? What is our heart's desire and prayer? Foremost in our minds must be the desire for truth. Jesus said, seek and you will find, and those who hunger and thirst after righteousness shall be filled. Prayerful, honest acceptance of the word of God should be the primary focus of our lives, followed by satisfaction in abiding in that light of life.

A great hindrance to receiving blessings from God is having ulterior motives when making our request. "You ask and do not receive, because you ask amiss, that you may spend it on your pleasure" (James 4:3). When our desires reach beyond the limitation of God's inspiration, discontent is the result.

"I neither learned **wisdom** nor have **knowledge** of the Holy One. Who has **ascended into heaven**, or descended? Who has **gathered the wind** in His fists? Who has **bound the waters** in a garment? Who has **established** all the ends of the earth? What is His name, and **what is His Son's name**, if you know?"

- Proverbs 30:3-4

"But exhort one another daily, while it is called 'Today,' lest any of you be **hardened** through the **deceitfulness of sin**."

- Hebrews 3:13

Between two extremes is where we shall find happiness and contentment. Unfortunately, through an insatiable appetite for wealth, many have pierced themselves through with many sorrows (1 Timothy 6:10).

The two things requested are for conditions in life that will enable one to live faithfully. All have this assurance from God (1 Corinthians 10:13; Matthew 6).

Deception, disrespect, discontent: a generation lost in sin
Read Proverbs 30:11-20

Disrespect breeds discontent, anger, and greed. Greed breeds deception and betrayal. Through four illustrations we can gain insight into the nature of desire. Then, through four illustrations we learn the untraceable steps of a sinner's self-delusion. How clearly these illustrations lead to the comprehension of the deceitfulness of sin (Hebrews 3:13).

The "four generations" is a depiction of every age and denote the consuming, progressive nature of wickedness (vs. 11-14).

- Disregard and disrespect for authority (v. 11)

- Pride (v. 12)

- Self-delusion (v. 13)

- Cruelty and mercilessness (v. 14)

Each step progresses toward a depraved heart that seeks no light. A generation consumed in iniquity will face certain ruin (v. 17).

"The eye is not satisfied with seeing, nor the ear filled with hearing," (Ecclesiastes 1:8). This verse provides insight in understanding the nature of human desire. Through observation of these four things, we can learn much about discontentment.

- The grave—Hell and destruction are never full (27:20; Habakkuk 2:5).

- The barren womb yearns for that which it cannot provide.

- The earth—though it receives rain, it will thirst for more.

- Fire continues to consume as long fuel is provided.

Likewise, indulgence in things of a sinful, temporal nature will not satisfy the yearning of one's soul.

Deceptively, sin committed in the flesh leaves no trace. Observations in nature provide a likeness of this phenomenon. This will enlighten our understanding to the fleeting nature of sin: "The eagle in the air, the serpent on the rock, the way of a ship in the midst of the sea, and the way of a man with a virgin" (v. 19). A solemn lesson must be learned. As eagles fly, snakes slither, and ships pass without a trace, purity can be secretly robbed from the innocent, but its ill effects are certain.

So deceptive is immorality that the blind sinner will justify his actions and say, "I have done no wickedness" (v. 20). The writer has identified a thing that is truly difficult to understand—the power of self-delusion.

Gaining wisdom from observation of things on the earth
Read Proverbs 30:21-33

Four things are listed relating to the actions of men that are troubling to behold (vs. 22-23). Then, the following observations of wisdom are of the least of earthly creatures. Though man has dominion over every living thing, he may turn and observe the activity of those creatures that he might better learn to order his own life.

As has been previously defined, wisdom is non-existent in the absence of practical application. One may know many things, but until one exercises that knowledge it is fruitless. Thus, we may observe wisdom in the least of God's creation.

- The ant methodically prepares for the future.

- The badger makes adequate provisions from the enemy.

- The locust, though left without government, works in unity and purpose with fellow laborers.

- The spider skillfully uses its ability to bring itself into desirable places.

We find in each of these small creatures characteristics which should be applied in our lives. Each one demonstrates a quality that enables one to reach that heavenly goal. Through application of these, we will find our walk through this life as one of confidence (vs. 29-31).

Memorize and meditate

"If you have been foolish in exalting yourself, or if you have devised evil, put your hand to your mouth."

- Proverbs 30:32

If, through observing these, you see your faults—whether it be exalting yourself or devising evil—put your hand to your mouth. Though we often seek words to excuse inadequacies, it is better to hold our peace and allow our conviction to produce a change of life. Certain actions produce undesirable results. So it is that the forcing of wrath produces strife. Therefore, whatever obstructs your assimilation of God's wisdom—let it go!

Questions to consider

1.   What state of mind is reflected in verses 2 through 4? _____

   _____

   _____

   _____

2.   Will God grant the two things requested in verse 8? Prove your answer. _____

   _____

   _____

   _____

3.   Relate the observations of the activities of the ant, badger, locust, and spider to

   wisdom in the life of man. _____

   _____

   _____

   _____

Reputation: The Fruit of Your Labor

Getting focused

A profound observation can be made about the identity of wisdom given in the earlier chapters of our study and in the closing lessons of chapter 31. Throughout the book, wisdom is referenced in the feminine gender. "Happy is the man who finds wisdom...for her proceeds are better than silver. All the things you may desire cannot compare to her" (3:13, 15). Now in these final maxims, real life application is made to that of a man who has a virtuous woman as his mate. The description of the virtuous woman will narrate all the qualities of one who has received the instructions of wisdom and is demonstrating them in her life.

Solidify a relationship with wisdom: judge righteously
Read Proverbs 31:1-9

Though our subjects have been broad and filled with many words, when this godly mother speaks she is pointed and direct. The son is admonished in chapter one verse eight to not forget the law of his mother—herein is that law.

- **Avoid immorality** (v. 3). Immorality robs men of strength and destroys their ability to be wise leaders. The ways that destroy kings had been demonstrated by Solomon (1 Kings 11:11). The strength to make personal use of his great wisdom was rendered powerless because of his attraction to those he should have avoided.

- **Avoid intoxicants** (vs. 4-7). The ability to reason and make proper application of God's word is impossible to those who are inebriated.

- **Be compassionate and merciful** (vs. 8-9).

These three simple yet direct lessons hold the key to living wisely. One cannot receive the wisdom of God unless one willfully rejects immorality and intoxicants. All the blessings

> "...it is not for kings to **drink wine**, nor for princes **intoxicating drink**; lest they drink and **forget** the law, and **pervert** the justice of all the afflicted."
>
> - Proverbs 31:4-5

God would so bountifully bestow upon us can be withheld because of being unmerciful. The substance of these three precepts are the things of which pure and undefiled religion consist (James 1:26-27).

The value of the virtuous
Read Proverbs 31:10-31

Our pursuit of wisdom has led us to an individual who is identified as one who possesses all the forms of excellence. Those who possess these qualities are equated with the value given to wisdom itself (3:13-18). Because of this, a trusting relationship is established (v. 11).

Memorize and meditate

"Charm is deceitful and beauty is passing, but a woman who fears the Lord, she shall be praised."

- Proverbs 31:30

As we have previously determined, wisdom does not exist in the absence of practical application and demonstration. The description of the virtuous women exemplifies wisdom.

- Trustworthy (v. 11)

- Diligent (vs. 13-15)

- Perceptive (vs. 16-18)

- Benevolent (v. 20)

- Courageous (v. 21)

- Not self-serving (v. 23)

- Strong and optimistic (v. 25)

- Edifying in speech (v. 26)

One's reputation speaks for itself. As was noted in 27:21b (a man is valued by what others say of him), the possessor of wisdom is adored and praised by those with whom she comes in contact. Though the wise are not self-serving, they shall reap the blessings from their labor.

"The fear of the Lord is the beginning of knowledge" (1:7). This knowledge must be translated into practical living. This is accomplished when we reverence God and His word by seeking to do His will. He has promised to those who, by faith, ask wisdom of Him—He will provide. "If any of you lacks wisdom, let him ask of God, who gives to all liberally and without reproach, and it will be given to him" (James 1:5). Having this promise of Him, we need only to search our hearts.

Questions to consider

1. What do the three admonitions of vs. 3-9 summarize? _____

    _____

    _____

    _____

2. What do you consider the most notable qualities of the virtuous woman? _____

    _____

    _____

    _____

3. Be prepared to discuss what you consider the most significant benefit you have drawn from your study of the book of Proverbs. _____

    _____

    _____

    _____

www.ingramcontent.com/pod-product-compliance
Lightning Source LLC
LaVergne TN
LVHW061328060426
835511LV00012B/1917